# EASTLEIGH

## A RAILWAY TOWN

**Kevin Robertson**

*in conjunction with Hampshire County Museum Service*

HAMPSHIRE BOOKS

First published in 1992 by Hampshire Books

Copyright © 1992 Kevin Robertson

HAMPSHIRE BOOKS
**Official Publisher to**

 *Hampshire*
C O U N T Y   C O U N C I L

in association with Southgate Publishers Ltd

Southgate Publishers Ltd
Glebe House, Church Street, Crediton, Devon EX17 2AF
Tel: 0363 777575  Fax: 0363 776007

SALES
Direct sales enquiries to Hampshire Books at the address above

ISBN 1 871940-05-2

**British Library Cataloguing-in-publication Data**
CIP Catalogue Record for this book is available from the British Library

Printed and bound in Great Britain by Short Run Press, Exeter

*Front cover:* Locomotive No. E850 *Lord Nelson* in front of Eastleigh Works.

Trackmen posed for the camera at Eastleigh, probably around 1900.

Leigh Road, Eastleigh, looking west from the junction with Southampton Road and the railway station.

*Frontispiece:* Railway and canal together at Allbrook.  A superb study dating from the later years of the nineteenth century when, despite being superseded by the iron rail, the Itchen Navigation still maintained a sense of dignity and proportion.

# CONTENTS

Introduction and Acknowledgements

# INTRODUCTION and ACKNOWLEDGEMENTS

It was with considerable pleasure that I accepted an invitation from the Hampshire County Museum Service to compile a book on Eastleigh and its railway, especially as to do so has enabled me to glimpse behind the scenes at some of the photographic and other items in the care of the Museum Service at Chilcomb – would that it had been possible to include all that was seen!

It was a pleasure also because Eastleigh is now my chosen home town, and although it has been so for little more than ten years, my wife's connections with the area are for considerably longer – she would never forgive me for saying quite how long!

I am very conscious, however, that this can be little more than a peep at the surface of the history of Eastleigh both in its railway and in its domestic aspects. Having been involved in the preparation of a number of historically related books in the past it is clear that to do justice to the area, in either field, would require a volume(s) of considerable size.

This book does not, then, set out to be the definitive history of the area. What it does however attempt is to present a brief and mainly pictorial record of the town, particularly over the past century, and in so doing, I hope, afford current inhabitants of the town and its surroundings the opportunity of viewing for themselves some of the changes that have affected their area over those years.

To produce even this volume without the assistance of a number of sources would have been impossible and I would like to record my thanks firstly to the Hampshire County Museum Service and, in particular, to Alastair Penfold and Gavin Bowie – also to John Gavaghan, a chance meeting which brought back many memories of years past – and to Hampshire County Council for their essential backing, especially to Stephen Adam.

Thanks are also due to Hampshire Books, and also (in alphabetical order) to Eric Best, Bill and Ede Bishop, and John Fairman – for much understanding, and of course Reg Randell. Also to Lyn for her soothing noises when the word processor containing the text 'crashed' and strange murmurings could be heard emanating from the study.

I would also like to thank those whose work has been reproduced or quoted from, including the archives of the *Eastleigh Weekly News, Hampshire Chronicle,* and *Hampshire Telegraph.* I also publicly acknowledge that I have referred in some detail to a thesis produced by Bryan Luffman for the Ruskin History Diploma in 1977 entitled 'Eastleigh – a home for Londoners in Hants'. Despite much effort it has not proved possible to locate Mr Luffman. As intimated, the records of the Hampshire Museum Service have also been referred to in depth and in particular the Eric Forge collection. All photographs are from the Hampshire County Musem Service or the author's private collection unless stated otherwise

Other sources quoted from are recognized national institutions, including the former BTC records at the Public Record Office, Kew, and also various items in the local history sections of the Hampshire Library Service.

Kevin Robertson

Part 1
# EASTLEIGH – THE RAILWAY

*Gaily into Ruislip Gardens,*
*Runs the red electric train,*
*With a thousand Ta's and Pardon's*
*Daintily alights Elaine.*

So wrote the great English poet John Betjeman, one of the many occasions he matched his talent for verse with his renowned love of railways. Whether Betjeman ever visited Eastleigh may be open to doubt although what cannot be questioned is the number of Elaines who have alighted at the station.

Eastleigh may not appear at first sight to live up to the romantic images of one of England's finest modern poets, but it does have many important claims to fame, notably its railway history, rich in tradition and dating back just over 150 years.

To the railway enthusiast it is names such as Swindon and Crewe that have long held the limelight as far as engineering prowess is concerned, possibly because these developed very early on in terms of railway history. Eastleigh however was a later addition to the scene, its first railway workshops, dealing with carriages and wagons, not appearing until 1890 and destined not to become fully established until 1909

THE COUNTY CHEESE MARKET FOR HAMPSHIRE.

AT BISHOPSTOKE.

◀ An early engraving of Eastleigh, then Bishopstoke Station. The artist has succeeded in capturing with some accuracy the railway geography of the period, even if the curve of the Salisbury branch is somewhat acute! To the right of the enclosure a long line of sheds is apparent; some sections of these are still extant in 1992. Although the Bishopstoke Road bridge is greatly altered today, the design of the station building can still be recognized, whilst all around is a green field site. This aids in dating the illustration to between 1847 and 1881.

◄ Looking north through the station, probably around 1880. The two footbridges are apparent as is the ballast covering of the sleepers – considered essential by contemporary engineers to ensure there was no movement of the track. It was later discovered that rotting of the timber sleepers could occur undetected. A side advantage of this covering was that it allowed a shunting horse to walk between the rails more easily; the animal in the background was possibly responsible for placing the vehicles in position at what is now Platform 2. Notice that at this early stage there are four tracks through the station.

*HMRS*

*The annexed Notice MIGHT be placed in all the Stations of the South-Western Railway Company.*

# To Sunday Railway Travellers.

The Directors of the South-Western Railway Company, desiring to relieve their Servants as much as possible from labor on the Lord's day, appeal to Railway Travellers, to refrain from travelling by the South-Western Railway on the Sunday, unless some very urgent call of duty may make it needful.

The Directors will, by Excursion Trains on the Saturday and Monday, give every facility to the Labouring Classes for visiting their friends in the Country, and enjoying the fresh air and beautiful scenery of Surrey and Hampshire.

34

# BISHOPSTOKE.

## DEPARTURE AND ARRIVAL OF TRAINS.
## London and Bishopstoke Stations.

| DOWN. | | UP. | |
|---|---|---|---|
| Trains leave London. | Arrive at Bishopstoke. | Trains leave Bishopstoke. | Arrive at London. |
| h. m. | h. m. | h. m. | h. m. |
| 6.20 Parl. | 10. 0 a.m. | 7. 1 a.m. | 10. 5 a.m. |
| 7. 0 | 10. 0 | 7. 1 Parl. | 10.45 |
| 9. 0 | 11.55 | 9.23 Exp. | 11. 5 |
| 10.15 Exp. | 11.55 | 9.31 | 1. 5 |
| 11. 0 | 1.40 | 11.11 | 1.55 |
| 1. 0 | 3.55 | 1. 8 Exp. | 2.50 |
| 3. 0 | 5.40 | 1.21 | 4.15 |
| 4.20 Parl. | 8. 5 | 3.11 | 5.55 |
| 5. 0 Exp. | 6.43 | 6.11 | 9.10 |
| 5. 5 | 8. 5 | 6.11 Parl. | 9.55 |
| 8.30 Mail. | 11.32 | 1.36 Mail. | 4.30 |

### SUNDAYS.

| | | | |
|---|---|---|---|
| 9.15 Parl. | 1. 5 p.m. | 9.42 Parl. | 1.45 p.m. |
| 10. 0 | 1. 5 | 6.11 | 9.10 |
| 5. 0 Parl. | 8.35 | 6.11 Parl. | 9.55 |
| 8.30 Mail. | 11.32 | 1.36 Mail. | 4.30 |

### Fares from London.

| Passengers. | | | | | | | | | Carriage & Horses. | | | |
|---|---|---|---|---|---|---|---|---|---|---|---|---|
| Exp. Train. | | Exp. Train. Doub.Jour. | | Ordinary Trains. | | | Doub.Jour. Tickets. | | Car. | 1 H. | 2 H. | 3 H. |
| 1 Cl. | 2 Cl. | 1 Cl. | 2 Cl. | 1 Cl. | 2 Cl. | 3 Cl. | 1 Cl. | 2 Cl. | | | | |
| s. d. | s. d. | s. d. | s. d. | s. d. | s. d. | s. d. | s. d. | s. d. | s. d. | s. d. | s. d. | s. d. |
| 19 0 | 13 6 | 29 0 | 22 0 | 13 6 | 9 8 | 6 2 | 21 8 | 17 0 | 33 6 | 28 6 | 38 0 | 47 6 |

▲ Trackmen, and possibly the ganger also, posed for the camera at what is believed to be the north side of the station. Each man is resplendent in the recognized uniform of the period, which included a cap and moleskin waistcoat. Manual trackwork was said to be one of the hardest of all jobs on the railway.

▲ The engineers' department weighbridge at Eastleigh, with the foreman, complete with bowler hat. Notice the screw jack – the railways were slow to appreciate the advantages of the hydraulic principle.

▲ The new bridge at Wide Lane which was provided so as to be able to accommodate a four-track main line. This was never undertaken although there were once plans for an expansion as far as Southampton. The bridge girders are hoisted into position by derricks with the power for these provided from a railway engine – out of camera - which would haul the rope away on the instructions of the man-in-charge.

when the locomotive works was opened – both of these are referred to in more detail later in the text. This, though, was some years after the railway itself had first passed through the area, 10 June 1839 seeing the line of iron rails passing south from Winchester to Southampton, part of what would later become the London and Southampton Railway.

At this time Eastleigh was a green field site lying in the shadow of its more important neighbour, Bishopstoke. To the west lay Chandler's Ford, whilst on the east, beyond Bishopstoke, was Fair Oak where, as with Chandler's Ford, deposits of clay had led to the establishment of a number of small brickworks. None of

The New Bridge, Southampton Road.

these was considered by the railway company to be of particular importance and, with no other likely source of traffic, there was at first no station or other stopping place at what was later Eastleigh. There was simply no need for such a facility although, as will be recounted shortly, one would be provided in the very near future.

To discuss why this took place it is first necessary to refer briefly to the origins of the London and Southampton Railway. The promoters of the line had at first been interested in connecting London and Portsmouth, although the reluctance of the Portsmouth authorities and in particular the Admiralty to allow the railway direct access to the city through the 'Hillsea lines' spelt an end, for the present at least, to such a scheme.

Instead, thoughts turned towards the commercial port of Southampton, at the time a mere shadow of what would later develop but still a valuable prize. In addition the directors had their eyes cast towards Bristol and accordingly routed their railway as far west as practicable, namely to Basingstoke, before turning almost due south across the chalk ridge towards Winchester and Southampton. Basingstoke was thus the intended throw-off point for a projected 'branch' to Bristol. Seen on any map, the most logical and direct route from London to Southampton would otherwise have been via Farnham and Alton.

The London and Southampton Bill was passed by Parliament in 1834, whereupon the company set about constructing their line as well as promoting the Bristol branch. In this latter field there was competition from a new venture, the Great Western, which had as its engineer the redoubtable Isambard Kingdom Brunel. It would be out of place here to discuss the trials and battles that followed, suffice it to say that the GWR won the day and the direct route from Basingstoke to Bristol would remain a promoter's dream. Meanwhile the final section of the original main line from Winchester to Basingstoke was eventually finished and the complete route opened to traffic on 11 May 1840, the delay caused by the construction of numerous heavy earthworks.

However, expansion in other areas was still very much in the minds of the London and Southampton directors who, as well as Bristol, had their eyes cast towards Portsmouth, this time via a ferry service from

► Aerial view of the locomotive works, in the foreground, and the carriage and wagon works, in the background. It is said the latter contained over twenty miles of sidings. Visible also are the various running lines and yards and an obvious expanse of housing in the area. Campbell Road runs up from the centre bottom of the picture

► The timber shop inside the carriage works, where, at peak production, two complete passenger vehicles could be finished weekly.

◄ Workers from the carriage and wagon works – again the fashion for headwear is apparent. Many of the men in the photograph would have been transferred from the original site at Nine Elms on which the expansion of the London goods depot took place. When the children of these men also started work, and later their own families, additional requirements for housing were created in the borough, and accordingly there was a large scale council building programme from the mid 1920s onwards.

◄ Carriage builders at work, seen here involved in the fitting out of a trailer vehicle from an electric unit in BR days.

► The decorative finish applied even in the late 1930s is visible in this official view of a Portsmouth line motor coach taken at Eastleigh. It was the practice then for the photographer to obliterate any unnecessary background so as to enhance the required subject.

across the harbour at Gosport. A Bill for a line to the latter town was more readily acceptable to Parliament and accordingly this was constructed and scheduled to be opened on 26 July 1841. Unfortunately, just eleven days before, a postponement was announced owing to difficulties with the cuttings and tunnels near Fareham and a revised date set for November 1841. This too proved premature and it was not until 7 February 1842 that the first trains from London were able to reach Gosport via a junction at what is now Eastleigh. Shortly before the opening of the new line the name of the railway company was changed to the London & South Western Railway, its new title reflecting the intention of the directors with regard to expansion.

Certainly by the time the Gosport branch opened a station had been provided at the junction, although it may be reasonable to assume this had been in existence from at least July 1841 – the month originally intended for the opening. There is also some confusion as to the name used at this time, with conflicting sources referring to either Barton or Bishopstoke. The subject of changes to the station's name is discussed later, whilst for the sake of clarity the more usual name of Eastleigh is generally used from here on.

Little is known about the station at Eastleigh as it appeared in those early days, although references to the stopping place do appear in the early timetables or 'Bills'. Contemporary press reports refer to the stations at Winchester and Southampton – the latter a temporary

EASTLEIGH LOCO: SHOPS.
Looking towards Portsmouth

◄ Construction of the framework for the new locomotive works, looking towards Portsmouth. Designed under the auspices of Dugald Drummond, Chief Mechanical Engineer of the L&SWR, the works displayed many principles of modern construction including wide and spacious galleys as well as good use of natural lighting.

▼ A panoramic view of the front of the locomotive works with the Portsmouth line on the extreme left.

affair at this stage – but make no reference to Barton. What is mentioned is the way passengers were '...whisked along at the unheard of speed of 35 m.p.h...', the lack of efficient brakes and any form of signalling to regulate the traffic seemingly of little concern to the first travellers.

From later information we can glean some idea of the original facilities. These were certainly impressive and reflect upon Eastleigh's status as an important, and indeed the first, junction on the L&SWR line. Up and down platforms were separated by four lines of rails, the two outer sets fronting the platform faces. The main building was on the up or London side, whilst access between the two platforms for both staff and passengers was via a board crossing at track level. The actual station building was designed by William Tite. He was also responsible for many of the other structures between London and Southampton including the magnificent (London) terminus at Nine Elms – this was

TWELVE O'CLOCK AT EASTLEIGH WORKS.

◀Gate No. 1 at Eastleigh, purportedly taken to show the midday exodus. This is a pedestrian-only access route which leads directly up to the bridge carrying Campbell Road across the railway.

▶ An early view inside the erecting shop at Eastleigh with a Drummond design 4-6-0 temporarily minus its wheelsets. Movement of locomotives in this way was by a pair of overhead cranes which ran on girders alongside the main roof supports.

before the railway was extended to its present terminus at Waterloo. Unfortunately the original Nine Elms station was demolished many years ago but its contemporary at Gosport still stands, albeit in very poor condition. The main station building at Eastleigh was a rectangular structure on two levels with accommodation for the station agent (sic) on the first floor. Above this was a hipped roof supporting tall chimneys. Between each was sufficient room to hang a bell, which it is alleged was rung to announce the imminent departure of trains. Intending passengers, upon arrival at the station, would enter their names in a book located in one of the offices, from which the derivative 'book-ing office' was obtained. It is known that the station also had a small goods yard, thought to have been on the east side, but early plans fail to locate this exactly.

There were approximately nine through trains between London and Southampton daily with the fastest of these taking some three hours. A similar time was taken for the journey from the capital to Gosport. Trains also ran from Southampton to Gosport via Eastleigh, although in this case a reversal was necessary and often resulted in considerable delays. A few years later Eastleigh also became the junction for Portsmouth with the opening in 1848 of a connecting line from Fareham to Portsmouth.

▶ For many years power for the locomotive works was provided from a small power station to the south near what was later the scrap yard. It was from here that the drive was obtained for the various shafts and belts. The equipment was coal fired and of the triple-expansion type.

16

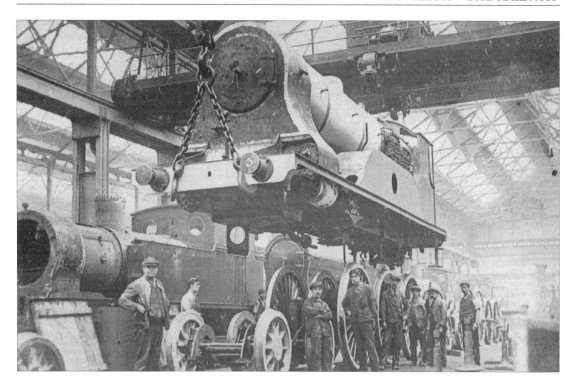

▼ The steam-powered traverser at the works complete with vertical engine. Two traversers remain although these are now electrically operated.

▲ A small drop hammer was located in the smiths' shop. The men here were possibly engaged in the manufacture of either longitudinal stays or perhaps even fire-irons.

◄ A steam-powered three-ton drop hammer situated in the forge.

Probably around 1842 an engine shed was provided for the first time, a small two-road affair likely to have been of timber construction. It stood in what is now the 'V' of the junction with the Romsey line, by the site of the present panel signal box. Further expansion came in 1847 with the opening of the line from Eastleigh through Romsey to Salisbury, although, as this was via a connection facing Southampton, passengers for Salisbury either had to change trains or have their carriage shunted before being drawn out in the reverse direction for the final leg of the journey. From early correspondence it would appear there was a suggestion that a north curve should be built to facilitate direct running from London to Salisbury via the Romsey line, but with the opening of the Basingstoke to Salisbury line via Andover in 1857 the need for this diminished and it was never built.

Shunting of loaded passenger vehicles was a common feature of the early railways, and carriage trucks were available so that more affluent members of society might load their own personal horse-drawn

▲ Believed to be another view of the smiths' shop, with a number of Urie superheaters on the floor. Notice the timber used for the works floor, which would swell whenever rain leaked through the roof. Some of the younger members of staff would then jump on these sections causing them to spring up out of place. Other parts of the works were also prone to flooding, in particular the pits in the erecting shop.

◄ Casting the inside cylinder of a 'West Country' class locomotive. Details have survived as to the identity of a number of the men, who include W. Lewis, Henry Clift, Geordie?, H. Lewis, Ted Ansell, Charlie Smith, and Works Manager E.A. Turbott.

► Inside the smiths' shop with a number of forges and tools visible. Notice that despite the heat only a few of the men are in shirtsleeves.

carriage on to a special vehicle and have it attached to the train. Surprisingly records do not refer to the fate of the horses themselves, so presumably there must have been horse boxes as well. In addition it was possible to hire, at short notice, a train for one's private use, perhaps consisting of just one or two vehicles and locomotive.

In the early days, rail travel was generally out of reach of the masses and it was not until the passing of the Parliamentary Carriage Act in 1844 that this situation began to change. The Act provided for travel on certain trains at a-penny-a-mile, as well as compelling the companies to provide covered accommodation for third-class passengers. Understandably such trains were referred to as 'Parliamentaries' and as time passed were often the slowest and most inconvenient services. Even with such restrictions travel began to be more commonplace, with the first signs of the rapid movement of population that is today accepted as normal. In addition, as trade improved so increased facilities were required at stations, and this was reflected locally in the developments that took place from about 1870 onwards.

Initially, then, it may be appropriate to look at Eastleigh station as it appeared around 1870, at which stage development was being considered in both goods and passenger facilities. Starting in 1871 a loop was built around the back of the northbound platform intended for the use of Salisbury trains, whilst extra

◄ Members of the same gang, again at work with a casting: *left to right*, Ted Ansell, Henry Clift and, in the bowler hat, W. Lewis.

◄ Inside the boiler shop. After 1923 Eastleigh was responsible for much of the new boiler work on the Southern Railway, with an endless stream of pressure vessels brought in for repair.

► 'Hi-cycle' drilling and tapping for boiler stays. Work in the boiler shop was heavy and above all noisy, but no thought had yet been given to ear protection.

sidings were provided north of the station. A most interesting feature of the period occurs on a plan of c. 1870, for, on this, Bishopstoke Road bridge appears as an underpass instead of the more familiar overbridge. The low-lying land at this point, allied to the length of such an underpass, would tend to make such a facility unusual, perhaps even unlikely, whilst no reference appears in the company minute boks to its replacement at any time. Possibly, then, a simple draughtsman's error.

At the time the railways had a virtual monopoly of inland transport and consequently almost everything that was bought in the shops arrived by rail. Large marshalling yards were thus needed to arrange distribution of wagons to their local destinations and Eastleigh, as a junction, and with no problems as to available space, was an obvious choice. Accordingly the east and south (Tipton) yards developed from about 1880 and at their peak were able to handle several thousand wagons daily with shunting continuing twenty-four hours a day, seven days a week. The opening of the north-south connection between Basingstoke and Reading had also increased traffic, whilst a further increase came in 1891 with the line from Didcot and Newbury which connected into the main route just north of Shawford.

At this stage it may be appropriate to refer briefly to the names that have adorned the stopping place, although, as intimated previously, there remains a

Members of the boiler shop posed for the official photographer in November 1937. A number of photographs of staff from the various 'shops' were taken around this time.

Knocking in and riveting the ends of copper stays on a Urie boiler. The men are using air-powered tools, without the benefit of any ear protection.

degree of confusion when trying to assess the dates of the actual changes. Following the possible use of Barton, Bishopstoke was the accepted name until around July 1852, when Bishopstoke Junction is referred to. There was then a change to Eastleigh & Bishopstoke in 1889 and finally, sometime after 1923, to just Eastleigh.

The rapid increase in rail traffic during the late nineteenth century meant that at times congestion was nothing short of chronic. Several suggestions were put forward to resolve the matter, which included quadrupling sections of the main London-Southampton line – those which affected the local area are discussed a little later. The opening of the little Hurstbourne–Fullerton line in 1885 assisted to an extent by allowing some traffic destined for Southampton to bypass the main route. (The Hurstbourne–Fullerton line was a blocking line intended to thwart the efforts of another company to reach Southampton. Its role as a useful diversion for trains able to run from Basingstoke via Hurstbourne,

◄ Believed to be the lower end of the machine shop. The narrow gauge railway was hand operated and used for moving heavy or awkward items around the works buildings.

◄ Inside the machine shop, seen from the boiler shop end, probably soon after the works themselves opened. It is possible to identify a number of components from a 'T14' class of locomotive whilst another feature is the abundant use of overhead belts and pulleys to drive the various machines.

Fullerton, Stockbridge and Romsey to Southampton was an added bonus, although full advantage was never taken of this feature.)

Surprisingly one feature never developed at Eastleigh was a flyover junction, although around 1893 this was certainly considered. On careful examination, just south of the former steam shed, a slight embankment can be seen which slowly tapers away as it runs east. This was the proposed flyover for the up line from Fareham and would have allowed trains from that direction to veer off before reaching the station and then cross over the main line by a bridge before rejoining the main line south of the station, probably not far from Campbell Road. Why the facility was not completed is unclear, especially as similar flyover junctions were in fact provided at a number of other locations, the nearest of which is still in use today at Worting just south of Basingstoke.

As mentioned earlier, in the 1880s consideration was given to quadrupling the main line south of Eastleigh as far as Northam Junction just outside Southampton, but again this was not proceeded with. A legacy of this proposal can still be seen over a century later at Swaythling station, south of Eastleigh, which was opened in 1883 with the main buildings set back so as to be in the correct location should quadrupling ever occur – hence the reason for the covered way linking the booking hall with the down platform.

► Axlebox boring in the machine shop.

PATTERN MAKERS' SHOP. LOCO. WORKS. EASTLEIGH. R.B. S. No. 8.

◄ One of several sports teams from within the works community: the boiler shop 'A' team – winners of the 1927 Mechanical Engineers' League.

At Eastleigh the station was partly rebuilt around 1895, when a covered footbridge was installed to supplement a similar open structure thought to have been put up around 1870. Regretfully official records are little help on this point. (The original open footbridge was still in use as late as 1920 but disappeared soon after this. It stood between the main station buildings and Bishopstoke Road bridge.) It is likely that 1895 was also when various additional buildings were erected on both the up and the down platforms, at a recorded cost of £7500. A little later, in 1920, some luggage lifts were suggested for the station but, along with a 1923 scheme for a new booking office directly accessible off Bishopstoke Road bridge, this was not proceeded with. All new works affecting passenger traffic had to be inspected by the Board of Trade, though the lack of detailed information in official documents is an indication that approval was readily given – luggage lifts were later incorporated into the footbridge although at an unknown date.

To the railway enthusiast it is for its locomotive works that Eastleigh is particularly renowned and perhaps to a lesser extent the products of the carriage works. The choice of Eastleigh for the siting of both these facilities is of particular interest and may be traced back to the late 1870s, when increasing constraints of space at their existing site at Nine Elms dictated that an alternative location be found.

◄ Pattern makers in the locomotive works.

► Axlebox work again, this time shaping the sides.

Several locations were either considered by the L&SWR, or offered themselves as suitable. In the former category were Andover, Basingstoke, Eastleigh, Salisbury and Winchester, whilst in the latter context came, surprisingly, Bishop's Waltham. Clearly Bishop's Waltham was rejected very early on, as was Salisbury, mainly because of the distance from London. Winchester is reputed to have been a favourite but here, although the local council was prepared to release land for the new works, they would not do likewise for a proposed extension of the station – it would be interesting to know where the works would have been sited in the city.

The choice fell then between three: Andover, Basingstoke and Eastleigh. Why Basingstoke was deemed unsuitable is not certain, possibly the amount of earthworks involved. Eventually Eastleigh was chosen. Accordingly the necessary Act of Parliament was obtained and the carriage works were fully opened in 1890, the Nine Elms site being given over to the goods department.

A similar situation occurred a few years later regarding the cramped conditions at the Nine Elms locomotive works. This time the choice of a new site was more obvious and accordingly these, too, were re-located to Eastleigh on land south of the Fareham and Gosport line and parallel with the main Southampton route. The locomotive works opened in 1909.

► During the late 1930s a small museum was established within the locomotive works principally under the auspices of the late Eric Forge. A number of exhibits were gathered, although regrettably the display was destined to be short lived with all available space and material required in connection with war work shortly afterwards.

► Locomotives receiving attention in the paint shop.

◄ Part of the tender shop with the erecting shop bay behind.

Coterminous with these moves was the provision of increased locomotive shed facilities, which reflected the additional traffic being handled in the area. By 1870 the shed had been moved from its original site to a position south of the station and near the present works offices. This was followed in 1903 by a large new depot on land which would later be south of the works; this shed was in use until the cessation of steam working.

From about 1870 a number of signal, or as they were then referred to 'locking', boxes were erected to control the traffic. The first of these were east and west cabins, respectively, at the London and Southampton end of the station. The east cabin was replaced in 1895 and then again when both boxes were replaced in 1905, on each occasion by larger facilities, dictated by an increase in traffic. These 1905 structures lasted until 1966.

Besides the east and west boxes a number of other signal boxes controlled the area in mechanical signalling days, including Allbrook, north of the station, Stoneham, south of the station, as well as boxes on the Salisbury and Portsmouth lines. The business of refer-

▼ An Ashford-built machine, No. A799 of the ill-fated 'River' class and named after a Hampshire waterway. This class of locomotive was rebuilt as tender engines following the Sevenoaks disaster of 1927.

*Continued on page 36*

▲ Inspection party of senior officials at Eastleigh with, it is believed, R.E.L. Maunsell pointing out the crosshead driven vacuum pump to his visitors.

▲A party within the carriage works. Such events were always held there rather than on the locomotive side, which was dirty by comparison.

► A newspaper cutting of the 'Legless Railway Worker'.

▲ Local Eastleigh tradesmen performing guard duty on the railway sometime between 1914 and 1918.
*Top line (left to right):* F. Hudson – fishmonger, J. Dixey – dairyman, A. Woodford – baker,
A.R. Ruff – jeweller, F. Budd – butcher, J. Collins – butcher. *Beneath:* W. Smith – baker, C. Stilling – tailor,
B. Brixey – baker.

**LEGLESS RAILWAY WORKER** sits down to his job in this special chair provided by the Southern Railway. He is Mr. F. J. Clarke, a welder. Formerly an employee of the company, he had both legs amputated—one above and the other below the knee—while serving with the Royal Armoured Corps in France in 1944.

ring to the boxes as east and west would appear at first sight to be a bit confusing, although it should be explained that the L&SWR adopted the practice of referring to a signal box nearest London as east and that furthest as west, regardless of the true geographical setting. In this way the boxes on the Salisbury branch and Fareham line were north and south, even if in true fashion they should have been west and east respectively.

Competition from other forms of transport was not really felt until the period after 1918, although somewhat surprisingly the level crossing at Southampton Road, near what was later the airport, was removed sometime between 1895 and 1907. One may reasonably conclude this was another feature of the intended widenings. Near the same site, Atlantic Park Hostel Halt was opened on 30 October 1929 to serve the large transit camp established on what was later the airport. Numerous refugees who had been made homeless,

▼ Volunteers in Campbell Road, made up of men retained for war service but training as 'Home Guardsmen'.

mainly from Eastern Europe, were provided with temporary shelter at the camp before moving on, many to a new life in the Americas. The platform, which was served by down trains only, was closed by 1934.

By 1900, train services had settled down to a regular pattern of operation with an average of eight passenger trains each way between London and Southampton which called at the station. The best of these took approximately one hour fifty minutes for the journey to Town but parliamentary trains still as much as three hours. In addition there were a number of stopping services to Basingstoke and Southampton whilst later, as traffic developed, there were additional services to Fareham, Gosport, Portsmouth, Brighton, Bournemouth, Weymouth, Exeter, Plymouth, Basingstoke, Reading, Newbury, Didcot, Oxford, Andover, Swindon, Cheltenham, Alton, Farnham, Lymington and of course the north of England. Such variety was often dictated by locomotive and stock

▼ Volunteers again, this time with a Bofors Gun, photographed in a field at the rear of the works.

◄ Amongst the new works carried out during the 1940s was the provision of experimental concrete sleepers with tie rods in the yard at Eastleigh East.

movements originating from the Eastleigh area and so meant the town benefited from a railway service far in excess of what would normally be expected for a community of its size. The freight workings were equally varied extending to a number of destinations both on and off the Southern system, but are not covered in detail here.

In addition to the freight concentration and transfer facilities in the area the station also had its own small yard for purely local traffic. This stood to the north-west of the station before the divergence of the Salisbury branch and parallel with Twyford Road. Here there was a large goods shed, overhead crane and a number of coal wharfs. Several merchants had wharfs in the area including, in the late nineteenth century, Messrs Bemister, Ulyatt and Cooke. In addition there was traffic

► The year 1943 saw the provision of some new sidings alongside Southampton Road and south of the station. These were intended to serve a dual role: to relieve congestion within the locomotive yard and also to disperse locomotives so that in the event of enemy action not all resources would be concentrated in one place.

in the form of general groceries, provisions for the town and an amount of milk traffic. Little reference however is made to bricks or sand being transported from the station.

There were also several private sidings, one of which lasted just four years, 1918-22, and served the aircraft park (later the airport itself), with access from the running shed lines. Another is believed to have been to the premises of the Fair Oak Dairy Company in Southampton Road immediately alongside the station and in what was later a furniture store. Additionally there was a refuse siding on the Fareham line at the south end of the works which was brought into use in 1929. Another siding was provided in 1924 for the Hampshire Farmers' Co-operative bacon factory (later Harris & Co.) just west of Twyford Road bridge on the

◄A long line of goods vehicles on the relief lines at Allbrook north of Eastleigh.

*J.R. Fairman*

Romsey line. Nearby was the siding for Mellias, Smith & Co. (who became Travis & Arnold in 1922), and finally in 1951 a siding for Messrs Combes a little further up the Romsey line from the Harris siding.

The railway company itself had also established an engineers' depot adjacent to the east yard, next to which was a signal depot, whilst a number of war-time facilities for loading were also provided. Further development came in the late 1920s when up and down relief lines were provided from Allbrook as far as Shawford, a distance of some three miles. Work on this expansion was authorized as early as 1926 yet it was not until 1931, five years later, that the new lines were ready for traffic. The long delay indicates that this was not considered a priority venture. In some ways this is surprising, for, although in the 1920s and 30s the motor car was at last beginning to have an impact upon domestic travel, the railways still had a monopoly over inland long-distance travel. Accordingly at weekends and holiday time it was standing room only on the Bournemouth line trains and consequently the numerous extra services then run required this extra line capacity. A few years later, in the Second World War, the new loops were used for goods storage, meaning goods trains would be queued nose to tail awaiting entry to the Eastleigh yards. The legacy of this expansion is still visible today when viewing some of the underbridges on the widened line. The brickwork is of quite different shades with the joins clearly visible.

► Adams' design 4-4-0 No. 571 outside the third locomotive shed at Eastleigh. In later years the glazing was replaced with corrugated sheeting.

*R. K. Blencowe*

► Eastleigh drivers and firemen enjoying a day's outing on the River Thames at Windsor in 1927. From the number present – over a hundred – the establishment at the locomotive depot must have been considerable to allow all these men to be off duty at the same time.

*Mr & Mrs A. Bennett*

◄Although it is mentioned in the text that the area has been free from serious accidents, these two photographs cause some dispute. According to the original text, the locomotive was involved in an incident in April 1908, which also resulted in damage to the house. No reference to this incident has however been found in either official railway records or the local newspapers.

A very good indication of the importance of the railway for the transport of goods can be gauged in a quote from *The Waterloo–Southampton Line* by R.W. Kidner:

'In 1932 it was decided that the Royal Agricultural Show should be held at Stoneham Park, three miles from Eastleigh. In those days it was assumed that most of the exhibition material and livestock would travel by rail (the previous year the GWR had built a new station for it at Warwick) and it was up to the SR to pull out all the stops. It was decided to build a new dock for the cattle at the Cheesemarket in Eastleigh sidings, and to work the haulage of machinery from Bevois Park sidings, Southampton. The east yard at Eastleigh was extended, but this was not enough, and the so-called ammunition sidings had to be used as well. The traffic normally using this siding was diverted to some refurbished old sidings near Micheldever. The road transport required to forward all the loads onto Stoneham Park was also considerable and a wide corduroy of road sleepers had to be laid right through the Carriage Works.'

▲ Eastleigh station frontage, looking south along Southampton Road. Almost all the structures and items visible have now been obliterated, the station entrance as recently as 1989.

Railway Station. Eastleigh.

43

A further indication of the amount of traffic on the main line may be gauged when it is realized that during peak times there was a *four minute* interval train service into which had to be slotted conflicting movements across the various junctions as well as various special workings usually emanating from Southampton Docks.

Also in the Second World War came the provision of a set of sidings alongside Southampton Road towards Stoneham. They were used by the locomotive department and ensured a number of engines could be stabled in the open away from the main running shed and hopefully less vulnerable to attack from air raids. Fortunately no serious damage was ever done to the local railway facilities by enemy action, although there were several near misses, one of which left two large craters alongside the shed entrance lines near Campbell Road. Eastleigh was certainly fortunate at this time, especially when it is recalled how railway installations elsewhere were affected, a number of railwaymen taking turns at manning anti-aircraft guns mounted on the roof of the locomotive and carriage works.

The area has also been noticeably fortunate in another respect, concerning accidents, with no serious incidents recalled in the immediate area. At first sight this may appear surprising as on occasions veritable processions of bent and twisted locomotives and stock have been seen arriving at the works. These often relate to incidents elsewhere, Eastleigh being responsible for repairs to stock from a wide area. Locally, a number of

▶Eastleigh station seen this time from Leigh Road with the passenger and parcels entrance visible. Much of the building work at the station was carried out in an ad hoc manner, to accommodate changing traffic patterns, and certainly in later years presented a shabby appearance.

lesser situations have occurred, including derailed wagons in the yards and shunting errors in both the locomotive sheds and the works.

But on 21 July 1883 this luck ran out when an excursion train from the GWR at Reading was diverted along a siding and then on to the up Portsmouth line to avoid congestion within the station. Unfortunately on the same line was another service, the driver of which mistook a hand signal for the excursion as applying to him. A head-on collision resulted with twenty-eight persons injured. Other than this, potentially the two most serious occasions were in 1964 and 1986. On the first date a steam-hauled freight train was brought to a standstill on the up through line with the axlebox of the third wagon on fire. This happened to be a laden petrol tanker, but prompt action by the station staff extinguished the blaze in time. More recently a piece of rail placed across the track at Allbrook derailed a passenger service; luckily the train remained upright and there were no serious injuries.

The intention of the privately owned Southern Railway company had been to electrify to Bournemouth by 1955 – coincidentally the same year as BR announced its modernization plan covering the whole country. In the event it was not until 10 July 1967 that the hiss of steam was replaced by the swish of electricity, although even then much of the stock was rebuilt for its new role from earlier carriages. With no more steam engines to service, the locomotive shed was closed, although nearby was a new diesel and electric service depot. The site of the former steam shed was adopted as storage for the new forms of traction. Just as the electric service spelt the end for the steam engine, the introduction of multiple aspect signalling brought an end to the familiar semaphore signals. A new panel signal box was built just north of the station and initially controlled an area formerly under the charge of no less than fifteen mechanical signal boxes. In later years this has been expanded further with Eastleigh responsible for an area from Roundwood (south of Basingstoke) to Brockenhurst, and from west of Romsey to Fareham.

The works themselves have also undergone a dramatic transformation, for dwindling traffic obviously does not require such massive facilities. Accordingly the separate carriage and wagon shops

◄Building of houses in Campbell Road, which was undertaken by W.H.Whitehead of Bishopstoke. The railway line down the middle of the road was provided to facilitate the movement of builders' supplies both to the houses and to the works and shed and was removed afterwards. Notice the kerbsides – fashioned from old rails.

were closed and all work concentrated on the former locomotive work. There was a fear at one time that this too would close but in the event it has become the main workshop for the whole of the Southern Region. Part of this survival can be laid firmly at the door of the type of traction used on the region, namely third rail electric, and whilst there has been no new construction at the works for some time, it does specialize in the repair and rebuilding of this particular type of stock.

On the freight side too there have been changes, so clearly witnessed by the almost continuous procession of lorries on the nearby A33 and M3 trunk roads. Allied to this, the closure of most wayside yards means there is little shunting carried out at Eastleigh and certainly not enough to keep a shunting engine occupied for twenty-four hours. Instead, freight is handled in bulk train loads, including stone brought from the Mendips.

But it is not all decline, for, in 1967, a new station was opened at Southampton Airport on the site of the former halt, but this time with platforms serving both up and down lines. This was later redesignated and rebuilt as Southampton Parkway and is a popular and successful commercial venture. Coinciding with the decline of steam, several of the down-side buildings at Eastleigh were demolished to make way for a modern prefabricated office complex. Unfortunately this was hardly in a style matching the rest of the station and externally has deteriorated so much that twenty years later its appearance is nothing short of shameful. The remaining station buildings have now received a long overdue face-lift, with Tite's original building restored to something more in keeping with its former glory after many decades obscured from view.

Part 2
# EASTLEIGH – THE TOWN

'A green field site in Hampshire', so might Eastleigh have been called, certainly up to the mid-nineteenth century. Previous to this the main centre of population had been at what is nowadays Bishopstoke, lying, like Eastleigh, in the valley of the River Itchen, which meanders its way south from its source near Cheriton to Southampton Water.

The Itchen itself had been converted into a navigable waterway in about 1710 and from this time until the advent of the railway was the principal source of transport for goods. The last commercial traffic used the canal throughout its length in 1869, after which it has slowly fallen into disrepair – the unfortunate fate of so many waterways.

Eastleigh itself may be said to have originated from an Order in Council dated 12 December 1868, in the reign of Queen Victoria, and was formed out of the

▼ What appears to be major road works in Southampton Road, possibly at the time the highway was metalled. The railway runs parallel with the road at this point and is hidden behind the wooden hut.

*continued on page 53*

▲ An aerial view of part of
Eastleigh with, it is believed,
a section of the Pirelli factory
dominating the scene.

► In keeping with its once rural
setting, this is Spring Lane at
Bishopstoke, near to its junction
with Bishopstoke Road. To the
left is the River Itchen – the
course of the Itchen Navigation
is some short distance west of
this point.

◄ The former Angler's Inn in Spring Lane displaying advertisements for Allsopp, Anglo Bavarian, and Devenish fine ales. The horse and cart would appear to belong Mr R.G. Stagg, although its purpose is unclear.

◄ Barton Mill at Bishopstoke, belonging to the firm of C. & J. Nutbeem. The names of both the mill and the former owner have been perpetuated in the present Eastleigh Borough in the form of road and estate names.

◄ The upper reaches of Spring Lane and with it the older part of Bishopstoke. To the right is one of many small chapels that supplemented the main denominational churches, although few of the former now remain.

► A final view of Bishopstoke and this time Spring Lane in the course of its meandering route towards Colden Common. The road has changed little over the years and still retains its narrow character even if motorists now attempt to use it as a short cut north to Colosn Common so avoiding the almost permanent road congestion of Eastleigh.

► Another renowned public house still standing today is the Cricketers' at Stoneham, although again with a far busier roadway outside. A gradual expansion of the parish of Stoneham has meant that this is now well and truly defined as Eastleigh.

◄ The northern boundary of Eastleigh may be taken to be at Allbrook where the farm buildings, hard by the railway, clearly date back several centuries. The chimneys are of particular interest being ornately designed in mellow brick similar to that found on many of the buildings at Hursley, a few miles distant.

◄ Southampton Road at Eastleigh with the station entrance on the right and hotel beyond. A number of stables were originally provided at this hotel although the area has been flattened now for a number of years. Few if any of the buildings now survive.

◄ The former Lloyds bank on the corner of Leigh Road and Upper Market Street. In recent times the building was demolished and replaced by a more modern structure.

ancient tithings of Barton, Boyatt and Eastley. Even at this early stage it is easy to see how some of the earliest names have been perpetuated in later area and estate names. Eastley, perhaps the oldest of them, was referred to under a different spelling in the Domesday Book.

In the 1850s the population of the area was little more than five hundred souls, who were at this time devoid of any church of their own. This was considered an essential facility and accordingly in 1868 the Church of the Resurrection was built to serve the area. The author Charlotte Yonge, who hailed from Otterbourne, donated £500 towards the cost of the building, and in recognition of this generosity Miss Yonge was afforded the privilege of naming the borough. Evidently the choice was between Barton and Eastleigh and, as recounted previously, it was the latter that was selected.

Much of the land around the railway was owned by the Chamberlayne Estate, centred upon Cranbury Park, and it was on estate land that a cheesemarket was established from 1852 onwards, just east of the station. Produce from a wide area was handled at the market and also from the principal local farms. Until the advent of the cheesemarket there were less than five hundred

▼ On the opposite side of the junction to Lloyds bank was the original Railway Institute – now the site of the bus station and Safeway supermarket. Here rooms were available for reading and recreation, as well as a large dance hall. In later years its main use was in connection with its licensed bars.

inhabitants in the area bounded by the railway, with most of these employed in one of three occupations: the railway, agriculture including milling, or domestic service. The railway workers were employed in various categories which included inspectors, clerks, porters, labourers, gangers, platelayers, policemen (later referred to as signalmen), drivers and firemen. It is not reported who was at first in charge of these men, although from 1852 this task befell the station agent – later the title was changed to that of station master – who with his family occupied the upper floor of the main station building.

With the workforce and population showing signs of increase it is understandable that a number of retail traders were established including grocers, butchers, a baker, tailor, draper, chemist and even an undertaker. There were also several coal merchants, brewers, a hairdresser and a shoemaker and, according to Bryan Luffman, an 'accoucheur', referred to as a male midwife.

▼ Market Street, looking south. The planting of trees – often limes – at intervals along Eastleigh's pavements was a feature of a number of roads in the borough. Even without a vast number of people present, the changes in fashion which have occurred over the years are apparent – shopkeepers commonly had blinds to their premises, whilst the practice of displaying goods on the pavement is far less common today.

Market Street, Eastleigh

Little is known of the first housing in the area although by 1861 the street directory for the town refers to forty-three dwellings, which included two hotels, one at the Junction and the other the Home Tavern in Leigh Road. The latter was one of the oldest buildings in the area. Three years after this, in 1864, a lease was granted by Thomas Chamberlayne to allow building on his land, the first stage of this new development being twenty-four cottages facing the railway and situated on the west side of Southampton Road. Less than a decade later there were over a hundred houses and by 1881 this figure had doubled.

Even so this was a small change by comparison with what was to occur between 1881 and 1891, for in this ten-year period the number of buildings increased to over 670, with a corresponding rise in population. Most if not all of these properties were again built by private builders and occupied by railway workers. The railway population increased rapidly as work progressed on the

*continued on page 59*

▼ A winter-time view of the High Street with the motor car replaced by a proliferation of horse-drawn vehicles – notice even the children wear caps. Stories are told of some young-sters eagerly running behind these carts armed with bucket and shovel, one way, it was said, of earning a small amount of pocket money.

Eastleigh Town Hall in Leigh Road, near to the junction with Romsey Road. Although now superseded by a large and modern office block some little distance westwards, the building still remains and serves as a useful home to a number of community-based organizations.

The recreation ground, tennis courts and bandstand forming the green which separates Leigh Road from Romsey Road.

▲ Flooding in Market Street in 1907. It was not long before this that proper water supplies and drainage had been made available to the town, the roads having been previously described as 'little better than open sewers ... a breeding ground for a potential epidemic'.

▼ The aftermath of the sudden snowstorm of 25 April 1908 which, besides the obvious effects upon the town, had severe consequences for the railway also. The view is of Market Street.

◄ The temporary huts erected near to Chamberlayne Road school in the 1940s for military use.

▼ Now the site of a large sports and leisure complex, Fleming Park was a recreational area from early times.

building and transfer of the carriage and wagon works, which consisted of six blocks of buildings and more than twenty miles of sidings. The cost of the new works was put at over £140,000. Despite such large-scale investment the L&SWR were reluctant to become involved in a similar house building programme for their workforce, contrary to the GWR at Swindon.

Foremost amongst the private builders responsible for the development of Eastleigh was Jonas Nichols, who hailed from Southampton – the Nicholstown area of Southampton is named after him. With the consent and co-operation of Chamberlayne, Nichols drew up plans for a large-scale development of the area west of the railway using the 'grid-iron' principle, with roads running north to south intersected by others, so forming numerous crossroads. Nichols then 'sub-contracted' to various other builders, who built south from the three existing north-south roads, namely Southampton Road, Market Street, and Tankerville Street (later renamed

▼ One of the earliest public houses in the area, the Home Tavern, in what is now Leigh Road – the original building is purported to date from the eighteenth century. The area of open ground beyond the inn is of particular interest as this has been completely covered by development for many years.

59

The after-effects of the fire in the High Street in 1910, when recourse was made to the railway fire brigade. Prior to about 1892 Eastleigh did not possess its own fire engine, although the works machine was later purchased for 'a nominal sum'.

One of several churches in the area, this one is St Mary's in Stoke Park Road at Bishopstoke.

High Street). In addition, the areas of what are now Desborough Road, Chamberlayne Road and Cranbury Road were developed, each builder responsible for various terraces of houses which were named by him. Most of these were dwellings for 'the lower classes' although, as would be expected, there was also a need for other accommodation deemed suitable for supervisory staff. Accordingly a number of larger residences were erected and mainly integrated with smaller properties rather than formed into a separate district.

Apart from the original residents of the area, Eastleigh was now home to a number of London families who had moved in consequence of the carriage works transferring to the town. There is no evidence of animosity between the original locals and new arrivals, although the first impression the Londoners gained of Eastleigh would have been interesting to record.

▼ Possibly the most picturesque of all the Eastleigh churches was the parish church in Romsey Road. Disused for some time in later years, it was gutted by fire and its future is now very much in doubt.

All Saints Church, Eastleigh, Hants.

◄The use of stone is again apparent in this view of All Saints' Church in Cedar Road and, like St Mary's, it remains in regular use.

▶Advertisement for J.P. Barton.

▼ A family group gathered around Frank and Harriet Martin of 25 Barton Road who, in 1897, operated a butcher's and greengrocer's shop at 113 Market Street.

Such an influx of inhabitants brought with it other difficulties, for there were now problems with an inadequate water supply and poor sanitation, so much so that at times the streets were little better than an open sewer. Again the railway directors seemed reluctant to respond to requests for help in preventing a disaster that could very well have also affected them, and it was only after a number of associated illnesses occurred that the council acted to provide the basic facilities of civilized life, today so much taken for granted. Until the formation of the local council in 1893 there had not been a body to oversee the requirements of the area, but the sanitation and water supply difficulties were then quickly righted, although not always to the liking of the near neighbour Southampton! In addition, improvements were put in hand with regard to the condition of the roads, as well as street lighting.

Despite this, in other respects the railway company did associate themselves with the well being and education of their workforce. A sports field was provided for

*continued on page 67*

► Tanner and Varnes' butcher's, in the High Street opposite the Post Office, which later traded under the single name of Varnes. The shop was especially renowned for the quality of pork and bacon sold.

▲ Hall's butcher's, which stood on the north side of Factory Road.

► Nosegay, tobacconist and confectioner, located on the corner of Market Street and Factory Road. Originally corner shops were situated at most of the road intersections within the central town area although few now survive.

▲ Display outside the Empire Meat Supply Company shop which was owned by Mr L. Hall, the goods on display being those entered in a foodstuffs competition. The photograph is thought to date from around 1900.

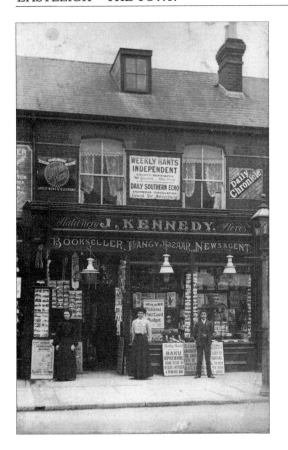

◄ Premises of J. Kennedy, believed to have been on the corner of Market Street.

◄ Shops in Market Street, including C. Sanger, Stevens, and the Imperial Meat Shop.

the more energetic as well as a mechanics' institute housing a well-stocked library, reading room, billiard room and concert hall. It was in the institute building – formerly on the west corner of Leigh Road and Upper Market Street – that classes were once held in science, mathematics and drawing. Education became a principal consideration, the first school not having been opened until 1871. This was followed by a number of additional educational establishments situated in all parts of the town.

Although most of this development was on the west side of the railway, expansion had of necessity occurred elsewhere. This included Dutton Lane in 1897 and in the following year what became the Newtown area. In the last year of the nineteenth century parts of Bishopstoke were developed on land from the former Longmead estate. Despite being unkindly referred to as 'jerry built' properties, these houses have stood well the test of time and the majority are still in use as residential accommodation.

*continued on page 70*

▼ Another Eastleigh trader, Pink, on the corner of Leigh Road and Market Street, who was a tobacconist and confectioner.

Market St. Eastleigh.

▲▼ Eastleigh's only regular cinema was the Regal in Market Street which, as was often the case, commenced its life as a theatre.

► There were several bakers in the Eastleigh area, this one being Harry Thomas Simmons, at the time trading from 92 High Street. The business was later transferred to 38 High Street and finally, after 1914, to 83 Market Street, where the son, Frank Simmons, continued trading until 1963. The site is part of that now occupied by Tesco stores.

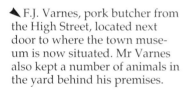 F.J. Varnes, pork butcher from the High Street, located next door to where the town museum is now situated. Mr Varnes also kept a number of animals in the yard behind his premises.

The transfer of the locomotive works from Nine Elms in 1909 led to further expansion of the town. More accommodation was provided by extending the roads parallel with the railway southwards. In addition, this time the L&SWR built some houses in their own right between the new locomotive works and running shed, in Campbell Road, named after the chairman of the railway from 1899 to 1904, Lieutenant Colonel the Honourable H.W.Campbell.

With a workforce which at its peak now numbered some 8000 men, Eastleigh had developed into a formidable area which in size was rapidly threatening to overtake its neighbour Winchester. Still, though, Bishopstoke and Chandler's Ford remained separate entities, whilst, further east, Fair Oak could be said to be little more than an unspoilt village. It was to be the arrival of further industry in the town in 1921, with the opening of the Pirelli factory, that once again prompted expansion. Allied to this came a new generation, born

► W.F. Palmer, baker and confectioner from Allbrook, about to set out on his daily round.

▼ Shops were of course also established in the outlying districts, including this one, T.A. Fretton at Allbrook.

◄An early horse-drawn means of transport recorded outside one of the churches bounding the area.

▼ J. Dixey, who had premises at 224 High Street as well as running the Bishopstoke Dairy.

since the first migrant railway workers had appeared upon the scene. Accordingly, further housing development occurred, this time partly at the instigation of the local council, who carried out a building programme in the Shakespeare Road and Twyford Road areas as well as around Derby Road. A few years later, in the 1930s, with yet another generation in need of accommodation, the opportunity was taken to purchase sections of the Longmead estate, whilst development continued on almost any available corner of land left over from previous times.

Fortunately there has also been an amount of care in preserving areas of open space: Fleming Park is still a valued corner of grassland whilst there remain a few brief fields separating Eastleigh from Bishopstoke. In other areas, though, the practice has been for housing to move away from the immediate town area, and accordingly whole sections of road are now given over to commercial use, whilst office space abounds. The

*continued on page 76*

▲ 'Dreadnought', a Burrell road steam engine, depicted in Leigh Road with what may well be a Sunday School outing. This engine is believed to have been owned by Messrs Houghton of Durley, who operated a sawmills, so the outing may have originated from that village.

▲ One of the first motorized dustcarts in the Eastleigh area. The letters stand for 'Eastleigh & Bishopstoke Urban District Council'. It is believed the vehicle may be of either Drewry or Dennis manufacture

◄ Eastleigh carnival in the 1950s. The firm of Lowman was a Southampton (Portswood) based bakery and operated a large fleet of vehicles on regular retail and wholesale rounds. They also maintained a number of retail shops in the area.

▲ Brick making at Fair Oak.

▼ Workers posed outside the brickworks kiln at what is believed to be Fair Oak.

consequences of this trend, which has placed further demands upon an already stretched community, are manifest in the huge new developments of recent times such as those at Boyatt Wood and Alan Drayton Way.

With a re-appraisal of the railway's needs, allied to changing traffic patterns, the town has slowly moved away from its image as a railway orientated community. The council is keen to attract other employers to replace jobs lost from the community. Compared also with the 1850s, few, if any, from the town are now employed in local agriculture or domestic service although, for the present at least, the railway remains (just) the town's largest individual employer.

► An unknown Eastleigh school group although possibly at Desborough Road school. Seated second from the right is Miss Miller.

◄ Class 3 of Derby Road Boys' School, 1912.

▼ Children at Stoneham School around the turn of the century complete with the then fashionable headgear and petticoats.

The Salvation Army premises in High street, Eastleigh, which were first opened in 1887. The building is now occupied by the Eastleigh Museum.

The original Crescent School in Twyford road, not to be confused with a later building of the same name in Desborough Road.

▲ Senior residents of Eastleigh, depicted around the turn of the century. It is a matter of regret that their names are not recorded.

▼ Compared with some other districts, the local suffragette movement attempted to maintain good relations with the authorities, as witnessed here in a cricket match involving the organization and the police for the carnival in 1907.

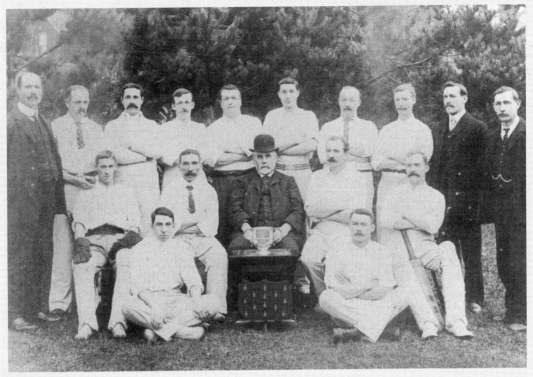

**EASTLEIGH ATHLETIC CRICKET CLUB.**
WINNERS OUTRIGHT OF THE CAMPBELL CHALLENGE CUP, SEASON 1905

Mr G. A. Purkess, *Hon. Treasurer.* M. Mycroft. C. Hart. F. Hillyard. G. Belton. A. Winterbottom. R. Darter. J. Truckel, *Scorer.* H Southall.

H. Bradley. F. Munday, *Captain.* W. Panter, Esq., *President.* J. Munday, *Hon. Secretary.* M. Rowthorne.

W. Mason. E. Riordan.

*Photograph A. Webb, Eastleigh.*

## THE FIRST FOUR VICARS OF EASTLEIGH

REV. J. THOMAS
(1889—1894)

REV. C. H. THOMPSON
(1901—1914)

REV. W. A. LONGLANDS
(1868—1889)

REV. R. C. M. HARVEY
(1894—1901).

EASTLEIGH PETTY SESSIONS.
*Opening of first Court.*        MAY 2nd 1921.

◄Celebration party held in the carriage works' paint shop in 1911 to celebrate the coronation of King George V and Queen Mary.

► Alderman Quilley of Eastleigh.

◄1953 Coronation party held in the Stoneham Hall on the corner of Chestnut avenue. Those participating were residents of Nightingale Road and Sparrow Square.

Best Wishes
Vince Hawkins

▲ Comedy in aid of a good cause, players and spectators from a railway millwrights v. electricians football match held on 13 April 1945 to raise funds for the Red Cross.

◄ Vince Hawkins, Eastleigh railway fireman, and amateur boxer of considerable repute.

▲ During the Spanish Civil War a number of Basque refugees were billeted in camps on the airport site. This was a transitory affair and the families and in some cases, sadly, orphans were later moved on to more permanent accommodation.

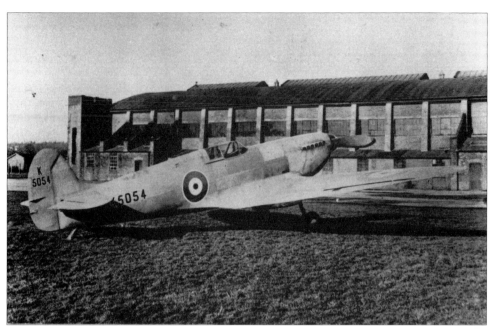

▲ A Spitfire outside the hangars of the airport in 1936. A number of these machines were built locally.

▲ A royal visit in 1943 with the Duke of Kent being greeted by an unknown man.

▲ The paint shop tea party, 1911.

▲ Rail and road at Allbrook in January 1960: a Western Region engine from Didcot heading south towards Eastleigh with a train from Newbury. *P. J. Cupper*

▲ With the station now looking decidedly dingy and unattractive, 'M7' class 0–4–4T No. 30030 waits at the original Platform 2 with a main-line local service.

▲ 'U' class No. 31618 on the 'up' slow line at Eastleigh during the latter days of steam working. In the background in Southampton Road are the premises of the Fair Oak Dairy Company – later a furniture warehouse. The dairy company had once applied for a private siding running across the main road although it is not certain if this was ever built. The scene today is greatly altered, the large gantry carrying the mechanical signals having been removed and the new Swan shopping centre and its associated car park dominating the skyline.

► Bishopstoke Road bridge and the line left towards Romsey and Salisbury form a background to this view of No. 30784 *Sir Nerovens* departing from Platform 2 with an 'up' service. In the background and almost totally obscured by steam are the main-line signals, their height dictated by the necessity to obtain a sighting for a train approaching from Southampton – the signals would otherwise be masked by the station footbridge.

▲ Another member of the 'U' class, No. 31630, passing the sidings at Stoneham – or airport sidings as they were sometimes known – with an 'up' perishables service.　　*P. J. Cupper*

▲ The final Bulleid Pacific steam engine to be rebuilt at Eastleigh, No. 34104 *Bere Alston*, depicted outside the works in May 1961. Amongst the group are a number of well-known Eastleigh men including:

*Back row (left to right):* H. Frith, ?, J. Miller, H. Riley, A. Bintcliffe, H. Pendry, R. Lewis, C. Matthews, A. West, A. Folland, C. Sharpe, G. Giles, J. Bentley, F. Ryan, E. Martin, G. Robey, E. Thorne, L. Bishop, T. Wood, G. Fenn, A. Graham, L. Griffen, A. Clare, G. Barrett, L. Smith, C. Spicer, R. Cramer, H. Fletcher, F. Riley.

*Front row (left to right):* G. Woodman, G. King, F. Janaway, R. Heal, S. Stone, ?, F. Service, R. Bolton, D. Dyson, L. Beasley, E. Harvey, I. Weekes, F. Hutchinson, L. Legg.

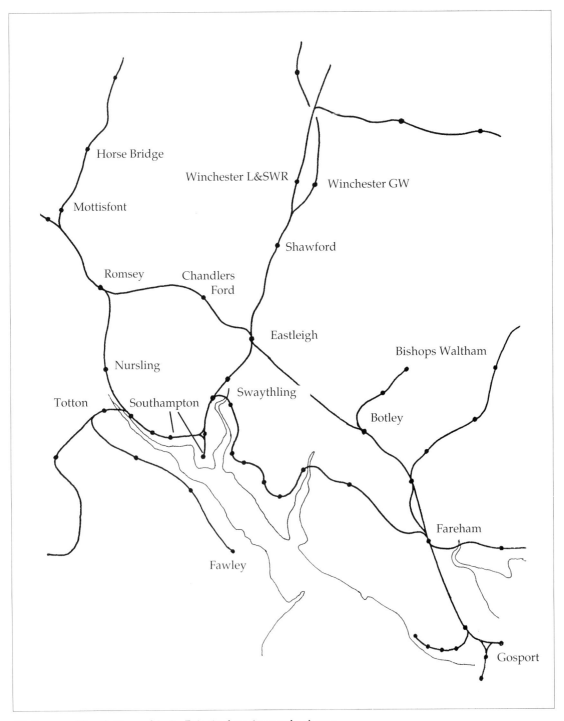

Horse Bridge

Winchester L&SWR

Winchester GW

Mottisfont

Shawford

Romsey

Chandlers Ford

Eastleigh

Bishops Waltham

Nursling

Totton

Southampton

Swaythling

Botley

Fareham

Fawley

Gosport

'Railways of South Hampshire' – Principal stations only shown

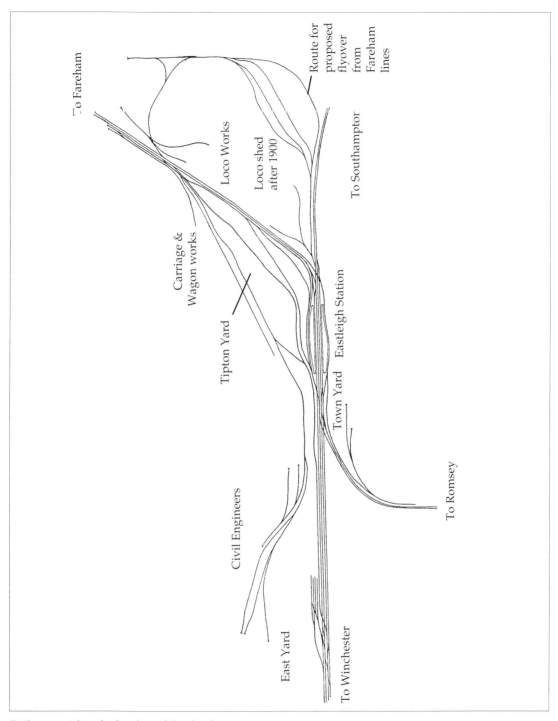

To Fareham

Loco Works

Loco shed
after 1900

Route for
proposed
flyover
from
Fareham
lines

To Southampton

Carriage &
Wagon works

Tipton Yard

Eastleigh Station

Town Yard

Civil Engineers

To Romsey

East Yard

To Winchester

Railways within the locality of Eastleigh

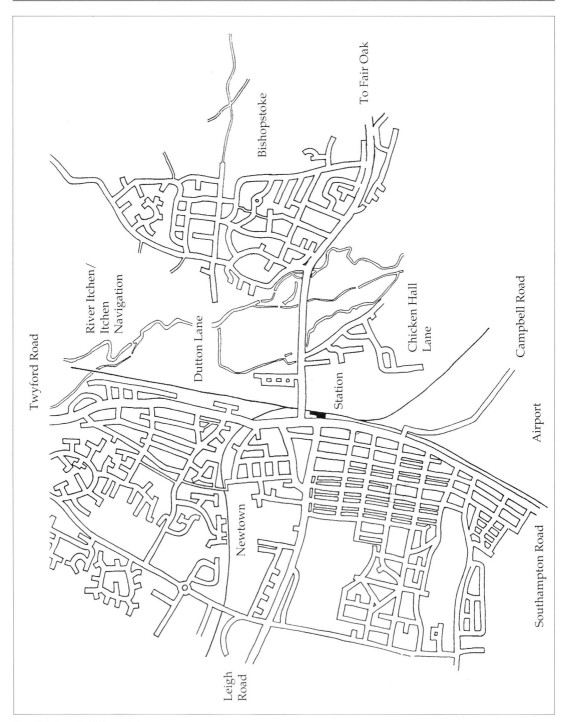

Eastleigh and Bishopstoke